7:45
BY THE
WINDOW

7:45
BY THE
WINDOW

A J I A H   J O N E S

WESTBOW
PRESS®
A DIVISION OF THOMAS NELSON
& ZONDERVAN

WestBow Press books may be ordered through booksellers or by contacting:

WestBow Press
A Division of Thomas Nelson & Zondervan
1663 Liberty Drive
Bloomington, IN 47403
www.westbowpress.com
1 (866) 928-1240

ISBN: 978-1-4908-6871-4 (sc)
ISBN: 978-1-4908-6872-1 (e)

Library of Congress Control Number: 2015901607

Print information available on the last page.

WestBow Press rev. date: 7/29/2015

For my family
&
To the wonders I have yet to learn

*Keep in mind that I'm an artist, and
I'm sensitive about my work.*
—Erykah Badu

BARE

Bare
Bleeding knuckles wrapped in winter air
Bare like infant feet
Bare like a first love that dances in the wind
    lifting the birds higher and higher
Painting the sky blue
This dream
Taken to Heaven with blistered knees I'd cry to God
I thought to myself, assessing the fact that maybe
    my dreams won't allow enough mutations within
    a nightmare to create something beautiful
These dreams
The fantasies that are realities in my mind
I hope that my child will dream
I wish to hold my daughter with these hands of mine
Mindlessly trimming the minds of mine enemy's
Because my dream is an unchanging effort, an evolving subject
With these thoughts
I have dreams
I wish I could hold them and tell them that it didn't
    matter if history repeated itself because it was
    just amazing the first time it happened

I wish I could do the things that you dreamed to do
    so when you opened your eyes rather than closing
    them to create a dream you would see me
And see it come true
I wish I could be your honesty
Honestly
I wish I could be bare for you
Bleed for you, for you to see that we are not that far apart
I wish to be bare for you
Bare like bleeding knuckles wrapped in winter air
Bare like infant feet

ONCE TOLD

She says my words do real stuff for her
Helps her fill in the blanks
Correct all the misspelled memories left behind from the last one
She said it reminds her of somebody she used to know
She said she was thinking about it the other day
The clarity that blossomed from the form of her hairline
It made her take away something from the
    world that could never be recycled
Small packages addressed for each individual
    willing to find it on their front step
Physically craving we're all chasing it
That moment when you realize that the real is worth it
Living in between the lines my honesty is good for it
She says my words do real tricks, far from magic
Somehow they move mountains for her
Give her faith
Make her believe love is real and that it could
    be the purest form of emotion
Keeps her writing marks on the wall because the
    broken windows are no better than the doors
My mind helps her thoughts
Unwind without a drink

Guess you could say this love thing keeps her alive
She's subscribed to the
Unraveling knots of my memory, which are beginning
    to find themselves in single strands
To be held in hands
Then transmitted to your thoughts she was caught
Held close by each syllable
Guess you could say this love thing keeps her alive

HOWL

I heard laughter coming from the broken kids
    playing jump rope down the street during the
    summertime when the flowers stopped growing

Who seemed to sing the songs that the birds never
    could because the students were too afraid to read
    them in the moonlight after the stars started to
    fade because they were mistaken for airplanes

They who could fathom the idea of keeping secrets to
    themselves but instead put it on their most recent status
    addressing it to the unknown name that we all know

Who will make the craziest and most unusual grandparents

Who thank God after every sneeze but fail to thank
    him for every meal, because instead we digest the
    latest news to catch up on the cutest shoes

Who cry on holidays since every other day filled empty jars
    with water and orange forget me knots and little dust
    assuming it would grow, because every other person
    who missed out on those days stunted your growth

Who fight the sleep of nightmares because it stings harder than
    reality, so instead pleasure themselves with the lives seen on
    the television a mechanical box that will soon break down

Who love words that encamp around the body
    drinking the night away because we have a
    thing for pleasure, a taste for arousing

Who think that resurrecting tried dreams is dead,
    anonymous mischief they dare not, tying all we
    are together I heard them breaking windows
    letting the breeze in, cleaning the old out

TASTE

His kisses taste like champagne to a court win
A first dance to a girl who took three hours to get
  dressed because her crush would be there
Like a road map back home to the lost child
  who only wanted to be loved
Like baptism to a saint
Like truth to a sinner
This is personal to me
A shooting star
A midnight train
I've never wanted to leave
It reminds me of love and sobriety
The option only consists of me or me
Choose not to celebrate
But you look delightful in your attire
Dance with me
Your kisses taste like champagne to a court win

BREATHE

Breathe and leave the stain of your breath in the
    mirror and draw in between the negatives
I have searched for you in your refection in the
    glass from the trail of your fingerprints
Your smile in the negatives
Each line releases another memory
Sometimes I pray for your shadow to kiss me
Dance with me
Your heartbeat is the perfect rhythm
Incision, perfectly dissecting night and day
    So I won't miss you too much
This decision to keep you has been one of simplicity
Its like breathing, it comes easily

REAL

Lets not act as if reality is really that far away
Because realistically we're just living our mistakes on replay
I think of you from time to time
Comes in a day dream
I see you in the mirror; I guess I see that part of you in me
Remembering the scent you left on me
The thoughts you said to me
The music you danced to
We used to tango and you used to lead me
I became comfortable self-governing
But you were more of the trickle down type
Then you left suddenly it didn't feel right
I guess the slow steps we took are now fading away
We're safer than the noises at night
And that's a scary thing
Certain words are purposed to sing
I couldn't conceal these insides
There aren't many places to hide
I cant act like its not real so you I would confide
Your eyes I shelter in
Your lips protect me from
Unspoken words of departure

Even my shadow is scared
You made me see things that were hidden in the dark
And remember that dreams are only dreams
    until I breathe them into reality but
Lets not act as if reality is really that far away
Because realistically we're just living our mistakes on replay
But I know the best of me
I think about it everyday

I hope you see a little bit of yourself
within each piece of work

HOME

I come from a place where they wear Gucci
    and Prada at the bus stop
And Channel #5 is quite reminiscent of coffee and cigarettes
Corner boys find stairways to heaven in the cracks
    of the sidewalk trailing to the alleyway that leads
    them to an angel dressed in black lace
More reminiscent of Hell
Where rain is more like tears poured from empty bottles
The closest limo is the town bus where you are
    treated like royalty Monday through Friday
The fakest in line kiss twice just to make sure
    they get both sides of who is really fake
And the last to be loved in the line are handed
    large portions of free honesty
Honestly rooftops seem to be the safest place, closet to God
Because they stole from the liquor store across the street
And the blinking lights are disturbing my sleep
I pray that someone would just turn the music off for once
So everyone could stop dancing to the beat
    of their own inconsistencies
Conveniently we're all just searching

Mimicking each movement to see which
	one doesn't hurt the most
Seeing which friendship doesn't cut the most
Which façade covers the most, they purchase the most
I come from a place where it all seems unreal
Because most think that the cracks in the sidewalk can heal
I've seen a rose grow from concrete it was beautiful
Much like looking in the mirror
I've seen very few places like this
That remind me of preexisting civilizations
Too reluctant to shake hands
We've all written survival strategies in our palms
Where each story is of home
Home

PAROLE

I am conjoined to you by metal
A black strap and blinking lights
You remind me of the stars that I never touched
The sidewalk I never kissed
And the memories I never had, despite a
    slight possibility that I could have
I could've kissed you and watched the sun come arise
    from sleep hiding under her black night sheets
Angels to sing sweet love songs as I wiped
    the shine from your brow
But my imagination has been locked away into a
    black box hidden right above my right ankle
I am conjoined to you
By metal a black strap and blinking lights

PAINT

Graffiti filled heart
Craving for that tagged sidewalk
Hidden from the law

It feels good, inside
My concrete jungle kingdom
Where I hold my crown

My pleasure is still
Nor rain nor tears can wash away
My kingdom Van Gogh

Speak to me right now
I live on the time, moment
When your lips inflate

I get high from you
This drug doctors have no cure
Adhesives won't fix

The first opening
Allows me to enter in
Emotions, you speak

UNTITLED THIS HERE

Too much of a good thing may be bad
Too much sun light in your eyes after dancing
    in the dark smelling the stars
Evokes some type of emotion I can't understand
Inability to comprehend
What does gunpowder taste like after wishing on stars?
I doubt that bullet goes very far
Too much of a good thing
Birds whispering on the leather of your eardrums,
    Biting away at your fingertips
What do you think about?
Thoughts laced in dreams of forever
Viewed on broken televisions how's your vision
    sleeping on top of rocks and stopped clocks
Stored energy shopping for patience in closed shops why
    act like you cant listen wrapped in a moment
Too much of a good thing
Is doing me a lot of bad
I told the doctor I had a heart attack
This he could've believe

Nighttime has changed the colors of the leaves on the tree
My back has been hurting lately, from the world's
    loads ever since I put down the wings
Have you ever lied?
Only on my right side
I once saw Mr.brightside
Like a rap song on the radio
My distaste for you bouncing in my ears as
    if some trampoline is growing
Was there a welcome sign on my shirt when you met
    me, or was my smiling inviting enough?
My eyes and hair flip enticing
Dance for a second, but don't enjoy it for forever
Too much of a good thing may be bad but
Somehow we enjoy dark weather

HIKE

We fall hard sometimes
Myself harder than others
Judging gravity

Season was changing
It was my time to grow up
It felt good to be

I don't want to talk
My thoughts talk alone
I know what I say

I like you I do
But silence is a pleasure
That I'll trust to keep

Hope that when I do
All is said, silence dances
In could be stories

Trees don't fall too hard
Unless your there to catch it
That's why God made spring

*"If you dare to take this journey
inside my mind be careful"*

NAMETAG

The entire time while you were talking
I continuously stared up at you not because
    of your 6'4 godlike height
Or your lips that I wish rained down on mine
Or because I kept getting lost in the sea of your blue eyes
But because I was trying to anticipate the next time you
    would run your fingers through your inch long hair
So that I could read your nametag
And hopefully search your name in Facebook and have
    your picture be the first avatar that pops up
I know our conversation went well because you came back
We talked and chatted and smirked and laughed
But forgive me for not being intimate
I just want to get to know you first
So I continued the conversation even if we both knew there
    was nothing left for us to say regarding the topic of college
So instead I studied you, and each hair on your
    chin that followed up to your cheek
I even studied your eyebrows and wondered if you
    pluck or wax because they were starting to meet
    up with each other, I even studied your height
Like some geometric puzzle I was determined to solve

I studied you like a moment I wished never to forget
And then your name
I realized it had an '05
So when you would look up or take a pause in
between the conversation I would try and count
to see how far apart in years we were
As if this could be a defining moment in me
figuring out this life long equation
I'm not that quick with math
I tried adding you in my life to see what it would look like
I tired considering my time spent with you
and what that would be like
And then I considered the drinks and overpriced
party sandwiches in the other room and
thought that may be a better match
But as I walked away still calculating every
possibility I thought to myself, yea
'05 must have been a great year

UNCONDITIONED

Love me as though metaphors are not real and honesty is
　　like an orange ladybug with 23 spots on its bare
Love me with that rare type of love that
I can't get enough of
So much so that if I were a non believer in something that must
　　be real for me not to believe in that I start to believe in
So much so I trust God because you were made in His
　　image that even the broken pieces of glass in between
　　your smile as you look at your reflection is Godly
Type love that
Keeps me coming back
Love me with that type of love that you cant sing about
　　because all you can do is hum and hold your arms
　　close to your body because its hurts to say words
　　that cant fulfill the meaning of the word
I can't believe there is a such thing as artificial sweetener
　　because the taste of you is sweeter than any pie to a child
Love me with those eyes of fire and light the flame inside me
Drive me
Not with the stick shift but drive me as in inspire me
Enlighten me so much so the sun is jealous of me, envy
Hold me

And let me fly simultaneously
You say it s hard to do all these things but I'm
    giving you a handbook to remember it all
Love me like winter spring and fall keep coming back
Love me like a promise you've promised to keep, as you
    rest your soul down to sleep and before I wake
Love me as though Adam never ate the fruit from the tree
And paradise was reflected on your smile with every blink
Love me like eternity was in conflict with infinity and
    decided to have a child so in order to figure who
    was more they had to find a higher power
Love me that power times two
Because I am only one person
There is so much that I can handle
So much that I can attain
So much that I can do with every gift you bring
Sing, like the birds that once had a home
But use their voice to reconnect to the disconnected
    landlines connected to home
Be careful what you wish for because I'd never
    kiss the cracks on the sidewalk
I'd never fill a broken vessel with wine

And love is best at its first and indescribable with time
Stop raising the standard of the painting you've painted with so
	few colors in your head stop you from tasting the rainbow
Because it tastes sweater than skittles,
I dare you to love me as though sugar did not exist and my
	smile was sweeter than any substance man has ever known
Love me as though you've known love your
	whole life and a broken home hasn't changed
	your perception of what it really is
And as if music or movies, books and tales haven't
	told you lies as to how to do something you
	already, innately know how to do
Love me as though metaphors are not real and honesty is
	like an orange ladybug with 23 spots on her bare

VALUE

You say you want a woman with good values
And a woman with curves you can value
Who values herself with high value?
Maybe even one who comes from a family with value?
But you've forgotten how broken you are
And through those broken pieces
Her face should accessorize the frame,
Cook
Clear mind
Love by your hip, and breathe through your ribs like Eve
Heaven sent, reminiscent of a fallen angel,
     but not too far from grace
Keep the peace
Appreciate the space
Pass time with minimum flames
Good with her hands so the babies can have braids
Extra accessories only when necessary
Comparing the physical to the mental

Is a comparison easily underestimated but weighted when
    determining the durability of the relationship
Can I just relate the beauty to the brains
    because they should be inseparable
But became two when she fell so hard from her pedestal
    that you couldn't even grasp if you stood on top
    of all the attributes you couldn't never have
Can stand the thunder and lightning during
    the rain and the idea of being wrong
Drama free
And keep singing even if the leading male forgets
    his lines forgets his placement overtime
Wearing masks of make up to make up for the missed time
But your daughters can't dress up their value in broken streets
That lay beneath broken homes because
    father was to far away father
So to take it a little further
She grows up disconnected
The tandem heartbeat between a man and
    woman have led me to dance

99 cents is not enough for the value of this song
Your worth and your value are priceless
But we've paid for you not being here
You say you want a woman with good values
And a woman with curves you can value
Who values herself with high value?
Maybe even one who comes from a family with value?
But you've forgotten how broken you are

DRESSED IN CROWNS

Catching all my dreams
Probably wasn't your dream job
But I dream of you dressed in crowns
Catching my nightmares too
Naturally inevitably you do the same too
Because someone told me
You weren't real
That you were my fantasy
But I guess some daughters don't realize that
    a father has the ability to be reality
That a man so beautiful could love me
And that his excuse for cheating is loving mommy Because I
    know there aren't enough good men like you to go around
So when you're not around
I speak of you on all sides
Sleep on my right side
Because I know you wont leave me
I looked at the photos on the wall and saw you and I
I told that girl nightmares weren't true
Because a man stood next to me in each and every frame
So daddy can you teach all your friends how to love
And how to envision vision
I see kings in my dream
Dressed in crowns

SAID

Overused metaphors are only for the things you can't really say
Repetition is consistent when you're lost
    inside your tales and fiction
Honesty
As many coins as you've thrown in the well don't
    suffice for the wishes that heaven wont answer
Switching your tongue will get you in trouble
Stop using metaphors
The way you despise,
Painted in frames looks as though you love every dying rose
Have you ever debated the unseen?
Your metaphors are only for your protection to
    shelter the thoughts you wish to hide
I understand I would never fall short of the
    memory; I'd hide them too
Dance in their broken shades of rejection but
    instead I've seen you hide in the light
In overused rays of sunshine because you're too afraid to blossom
So you overuse metaphors only for the things you cant say

ISSUES

She has more issues than a magazine stand
An open book
She only dates the finest guys
Her excuse is that she's trying to get it right, and the
     first time usually isn't usually the right time
But I can see past it in the daytime with a flashlight
She drinks rainbows with raindrops around
     the rim to change her tone
But she still sounds the same, like dry
     hair going through a comb
I figured the loudest ones had it the worst
And that maybe the furthest on the spectrum of
     character and facial features had the curse
But so much game rehearsed
Flashing lights in the bathroom
Nobody's perfect
I understand your pain
Reading so many books wont give you a better
     understanding of this lifetime
Laughing on the rooftops without you don't seem the same

Never forget your first name
But the grays get died out
Maybe I tried to hard
Had it all in my hand maybe it just wasn't the card
Or the face for that play
But either way I've noticed that
Expectations aren't high enough for my heals
And bold enough for the color on my toes
I've walked a few blocks only to find that
    outside is still out of control
Have you solved your problem the math
    equation you were dealing with
Have you said your goodbyes and given your last kiss
I have
4 pages, four tears
Wrapped in sheets of late nights and later mornings
Which is changing my concept of relativity
I know yours has changed

WAIT

How rich are you?
I'm going to make you want something for
    so long that you no longer want it
No mater how long it takes
And If I had told you from the beginning that this was the plan
    would you have lied to yourself to make time go faster
Or taken in time with welcoming arms as if it
    could be your remedy to a broken desire
I'm going to do this because it is what you need
And what you want does not suffice the glow in your eyes
Or the many tries you've taken to get here
What you will settle for is not enough for me
Because I'm trying to give you more than enough
    and more than what you deserve
Because if you were given what you are
    deserved in measure to yourself
Your imagination would be left to equal your wealth

Do You

I don't understand,
Looking in the mirror taking a glimpse away from Hell
Have you not glared at mirror lately?
Seen your face in the reflection of a car that passes by in
    the late hour as you wait for someone to love you
Have you never seen your eyes in the reflection
    of the windows as you shop for a dress that
    you'll only wear when you're sleeping
Eyes closed tight so much so maybe you'll
    think that you're dreaming
Like you get any sleep in
Have you never even seen your reflection in the puddles
    of tears that you've cried that glisten underneath your
    toes as you stroke your feet amongst God's earth
He left it for you
You fallen angel
Have you not seen what I have seen?
Or have you been rubbing the crust from your eyes
Ashes from burned lovers
Who said that they would protect you from burns left behind
Have you not seen what you look like?
What you really look like

I assume every one has told you what they see their
    perception but my God have you never looked
I understand that big girls need love too
But have you not even looked at your hands
Because obviously if you hold them out
We can both look at the same thing together
And then I would know you see them same thing I do
So you cant lie to me and tell me you haven't seen a fraction of
    beauty because I see a whole lot of it when I look at you
You look like me
And I know it's not a lie I am beauty
I am a King and Queen fused together to
    create celestial stars when I breathe
Have you ever kissed a slain dragon and tasted fire?
It tastes like the look you give yourself when you saw
    the raising mountains from your cheekbones
Looking in the mirror helps to take a glimpse away from Hell
Have you ever tried?

WONDER

I wonder how many iridescent shades the rainbow holds to
    make earth glow after a night of the heavens crying
Stain the lights in the sky over my daydreams
I wonder what it would be like without the reds in the rainbow
Would I ever know the color that bleeds silent
    screams of a motherless child who was fathered
    by the corner boys and hip-hop?
Without the deepest blues and the softest indigo
    the sea reflecting back my face the 75 percent
    of water that accounts for my shape
What would it be like without the seasons
    changing this lifetime rearranging?
Each layer your too afraid to peel away
I wonder what it would be without one less color in the rainbow
Would you glow like you do?
One less person,
Would you really miss me?

Is it only me?
Trying to wash off the paint
Of all my colors

I've seen as you paint
And color yourself
White while your blood is black

Even though the blind see
The colors orbiting from
Picasso soul

Midnight

As sober as I was I fell in love with midnight
His name was a Friday night
Hands loose around the bass in the dj's every song
Night air clenched to my waist loosening my hair
I was taught better than that
But I was taught to love
And I fell in love with midnight
I tripped on the beat and fell into warm
    arms heated from the moon
Starry eyes, cosmic lips
I chose my words carefully
Only used 3
The night grew old
We danced in black and white
Fingerprints intermixed with diamonds
Sheeting the rim of every drink
As sober as I was I fell in love with midnight

MY STORY IN A LATE STYLE OF "HEALS"

Whenever I listen to the conversation of the persistent
    window shopper my laughter dances
And I am reminded that the same story applies to the
    poorest of us who are wealthy in everything but spirit
If somehow you knew that the breaking bricks
    underneath your feet were unreal would you
    continue walking in the same way?
I tried running once I got tired twice I think I missed out
    on what I could have seen if I hadn't stop three times
It's a mystery how all this is available to me, I guess the problem
    is keeping it when you have it and never letting it leave
Shattered glass on the sidewalk, staring at the reflection in the
    broken bottles you could find forgiveness in every sip
I bet you walk differently now
I've been walking in the same way as I did when I
    came from home, a walk that carried me a few
    steps further than I thought I would go
How long does it take for a cut to heal for aloe to soothe a
    burn for the blood to stop dripping from an open cut?
If my feet start to hurt, I inhale the healing process and
    consider the future from thinking about forever

However
Don't get upset over the shoelaces knowing the
    replaceable is only a few feet away
You are so easily influenced, you let the tapping
    of my fingers change your mood
Torn soles from late nights, date nights,
    eating everything in sight
Sandwiched between the sole of my foot
    and the ground beneath me
I wonder how long it has been
Left you years ago. It is so American easy consumption to
    make up for the lack of make up cover girl cant cover
So like us
It get's cold sometimes, in its consequent brief triumph

THERE HE STAYS

I told him to walk away
He listened
I told him to visit me
He behaved
I thought it over and wanted to know why he was
    so keen on listening to my every command
He thought my voice was beautiful
The most harmonious sound he had ever
    heard in sync with my heartbeat
So he came back to visit me, and there he listened
Walked right into my palms, and there he stays

BOTTLE

Many pages of continually written stories lie in the
    bottles underneath the skirt of her bed
Staying up late into the night as if the moon owes her
    something and midnight doesn't scare her
She's learned from so many textbooks she disregards
    how people read the cards dealt to her
I've seen a poker face is tattooed on her smile
Newborn innocence has drifted far from her pedestal and the
    taste of milk has evaporated from the rim of a sippy cup
But have you ever opened a freshly finished
    dishwasher when the steam rises
Her shadow is seen through the windows at night
    when she's done cleaning the kitchen
I've heard her say so kindly "I thought you were coming back so
    I waited up for you, but when the moonlight laid beside my
    bed before you I sometimes find myself consuming little bit"
Sometime
Anytime
And now any time seems like the right time for a story

Life and Death are in the power of the tongue
and they that love it shall eat the fruit thereof.
—Proverbs 18:21

Printed in the United States
By Bookmasters